Poetry by Clive Blake
Images by Chris Robbins

AND
POINTS
OFVIEW
VIEW
POINTS

First published in 2009
by Emu House Publications
www.emuhouse.co.uk

Printed in Great Britain by Butler Tanner & Dennis Ltd
www.butlertanneranddennis.com

Layout and design by Adrian Blake
www.adrianblakedesign.co.uk

ISBN 978-0-9560724-0-5

Acknowledgements
We would both like to thank everyone; family, friends and others, who have given their help and encouragement. This book would not have been possible without it. Special thanks must go to Adrian, whose layout and design was the final ingredient needed to pull the whole thing together. Special thanks also to all those people, young and old, featured within the book's images.

CLIVE BLAKE

I describe myself both as a Poetic Punster and as a Performance Poet, since a lot of my poetry likes to explore the punnier side of life and I like to show that poetry needn't be restricted to the written page, but can also come alive as a form of entertainment.

I have had poems published in more than sixty different book anthologies and entered over fifty poems into Music and Speech Festivals to have critical feedback from nationally and internationally accredited judges. These poems have mainly been given distinction markings. Over the years I have been encouraged by many people to publish a book of my poems, but with so many poetry books being produced, I wanted to do something different.
The concept of making it into a joint project by combining my poetry with Chris's inspirational photographs has made the process more complicated logistically, but has also made it much more enjoyable and worthwhile.

CHRIS ROBBINS MPAGB,AFIAP.

I took up photography in the late 1970s, when my love of wildlife and the natural world gave me the urge to record its beauty on film. After joining Launceston camera club I began entering competitions and started working through the PAGB (Photographic Alliance of Great Britain) awards, achieving Master status in 2004.

In recent years I have moved on to the International circuit. Between 2005 and 2007 in the Austrian Super Circuit, which receives over fifty thousand entries from more than seventy-five countries, I won one silver and three gold medals. My entry in the 2007 Royal Photographic Society's International Projected Images competition brought me gold medal position. In 2008 I achieved AFIAP (Artiste Federation Internationale de l`Art Photographique) status.

I'm a great fan of *Clive Live,* watching Clive performing his poetry in his own animated and infectious style. It has been a really challenging and enjoyable experience taking images to illustrate his excellent poems.

CONTENTS

THE END

I began a poem by writing its end,
Like gunpowder exploding
Before the touch-paper is lit,
I finished that poem,
Before I'd started it ...

THE NEW MILLENNIUM
2000

A billion people partied,
A billion people danced,
A billion people watched,
A billion stood entranced,
A billion people smiled,
A billion people sang,
A billion people cheered,
When the new millennium began.

A billion fireworks exploded,
Like a global starting gun,
So no one could miss the fact that
The new millennium had begun.

On this first day of January,
There's more hope than ever before,
That the world can all push together,
On an already half-open door.

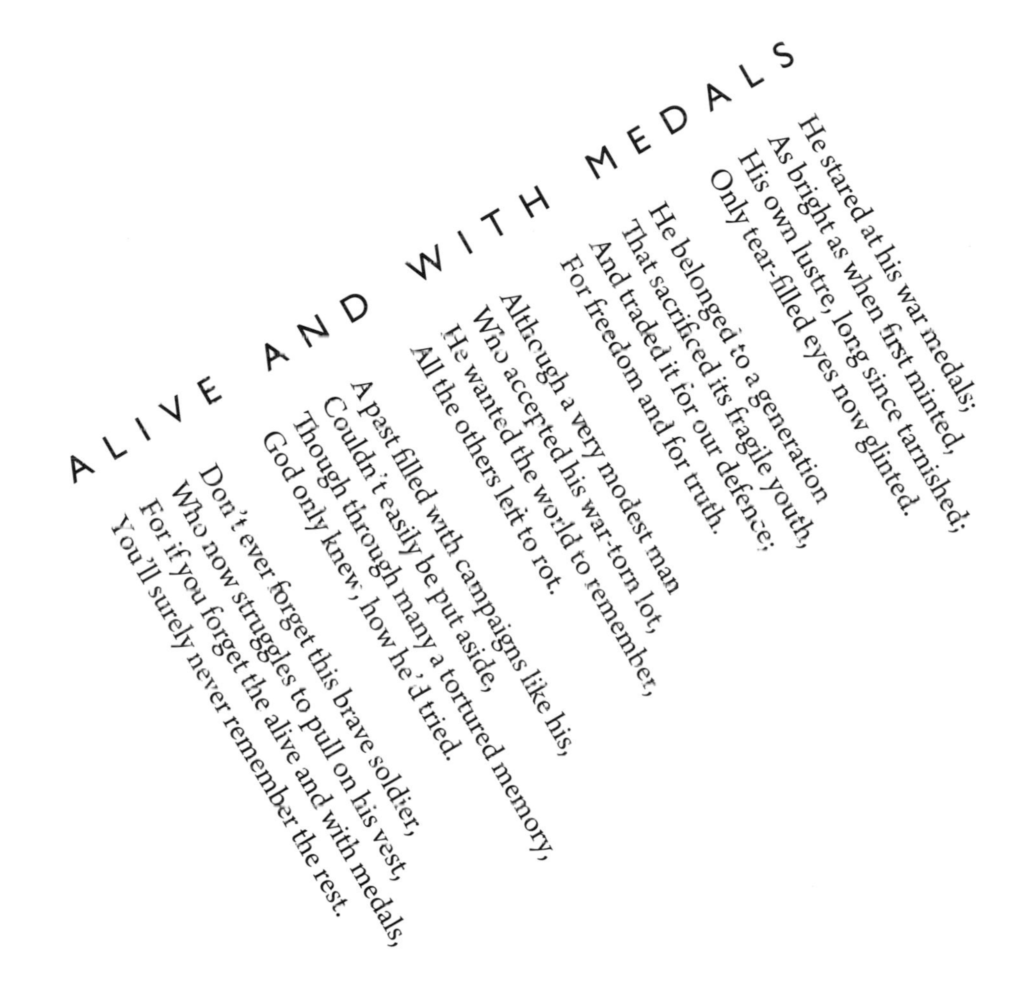

ALIVE AND WITH MEDALS

He stared at his war medals;
As bright as when first minted,
His own lustre, long since tarnished,
Only tear-filled eyes now glinted.

He belonged to a generation
That sacrificed its fragile youth,
And traded it for our defence;
For freedom and for truth.

Although a very modest man
Who accepted his war-torn lot,
He wanted the world to remember,
All the others left to rot.

A past filled with campaigns like his,
Couldn't easily be put aside,
Though through many a tortured memory,
God only knew, how he'd tried.

Don't ever forget this brave soldier,
Who now struggles to pull on his vest,
For if you forget the alive and with medals,
You'll surely never remember the rest.

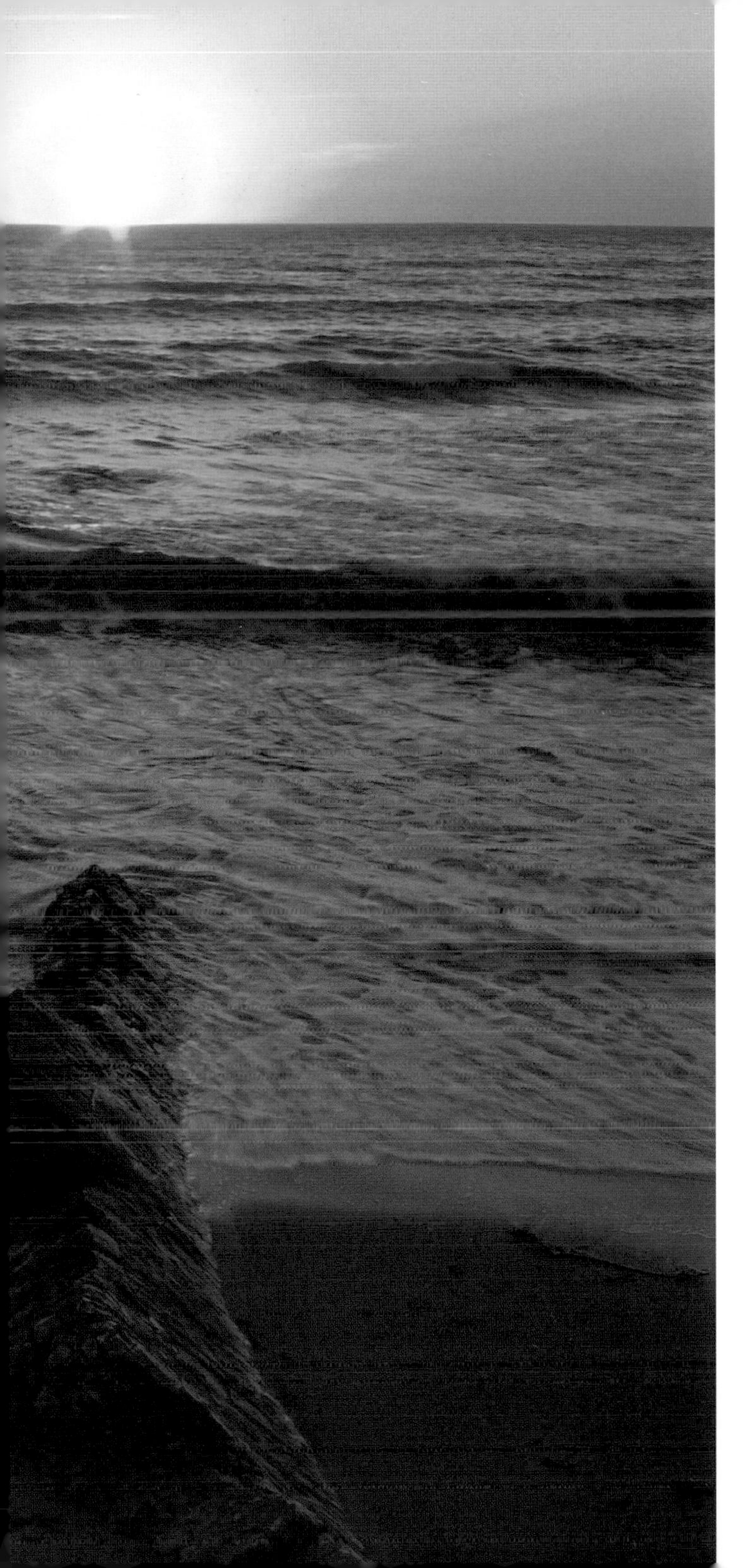

EBB AND FLOW

The seasons come,
And the seasons go,
The seasons ebb,
And the seasons flow.

The spring green hue,
The rich autumn gold,
The clear summer blue,
The grey winter cold.

The changing mask
Of our Mother Earth,
Winter her death,
And spring her re-birth.

Spring starts the tune,
Autumn beats the time,
Summer sings the song,
Winter blows the chime.

The seasons change,
Yet all stay the same,
Nature's illusion;
Her own magic game.

The seasons come,
And the seasons go,
The seasons ebb,
And the seasons flow ...

LICHEN LADEN GRANITE CROSS

LICHEN laden, granite cross,
Reminder of a celtic culture's loss,
An icon to placate a harsh deity,
A religious symbol, an outward plea.

LADEN cross, granite lichen,
Not a mere whim, but a deliberate decision,
Ley-line power, here to focus,
Awaiting another mid-summer solstice.

GRANITE cross, lichen laden,
Sculptured for a dark-haired maiden,
Elaborate and ultimate statement of love,
A prayer for a union to be blessed from above.

CROSS, lichen laden, granite
Manufactured on a far off planet,
Crafted and left to become immortal,
Marker of a time traveller's portal.

STRINGS OF HER HARP

She tickled the harp's ribs;
As if it were a young child,
The notes escaped giggling;
The harp happy and beguiled.

Notes so silkily smooth,
None too flat or too sharp,
As her fingers flowed like liquid
Over the strings of her harp.

Notes twinkling like the stars
From the dark heavens above,
Winging their way skywards as if
Chased by a white dove.

Notes deceptively simple,
Yet so perfectly placed,
Music freed now forever;
Never again to be traced ...

SLEEPY TOT

Sleepy tot,
Tucked in tight,
Slumber sound,
Till morning light.

NO MALICE SHOWN

See the owl in swift silent flight,
Surfing the darkness of the night,
In control of its black domain,
Its prey killed quick, no time for pain.

Don't be outraged when its victim dies;
The owl's not a mugger of the skies,
No malice shown when it hunts for meat,
It leaves alone what it cannot eat!

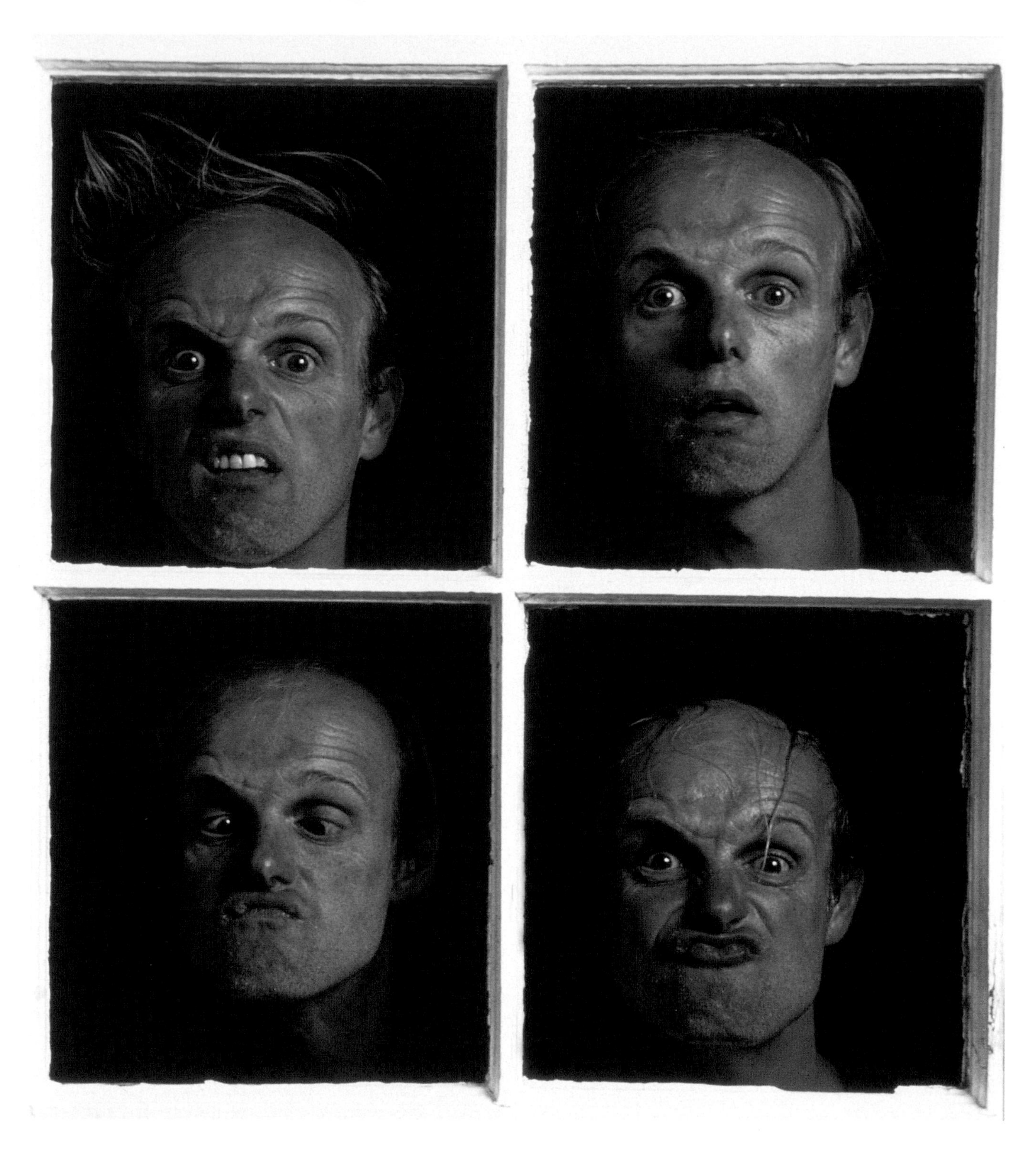

WHO IS THAT STRANGE OLD MAN?

I'm staring at this old man,
The old man's staring back,
His eyes are dull and misty,
His skin is weathered and slack,
Most of his teeth are missing,
And his cheeks are all caved in,
He has tufts of fluffy grey stuff,
Where the hair on his head
Had once been.

Who is that strange old man,
And why, oh why, does he stare,
Where on earth has he come from,
And how did he get over there?

He has the neck of a vulture,
His shoulders are feeble and round,
Decades of gravity have bent him,
Till his head is close to the ground,
His ears are as thin as paper,
His veins are showing through,
His nostrils are like forests where all
His hair has migrated to,
His body is skeleton thin,
His ribs are all open-plan,
There's something rather pathetic,
About this strange old man.

His stare is quite unnerving,
It fixes me to the spot,
As if he remembers something,
Which I have certainly not,
He surely can't have anything
At all to do with me,
He looks well over ninety ...
And I feel like twenty-three.

Suddenly a voice comes from nowhere ...
"Come on Dad you old fool,
You've been ages in the bathroom,
And I've got to get to school!"
Oh drat my failing memory,
How fuddle-headed can I be?
That old man staring from the mirror ...

Why of course - *now* I remember

it's *me*!

IN CARDBOARD BOXES

People living in cardboard boxes ...
What are they doing there,
Are they there out of choice,
Or there in despair?

Are they there through their own fault,
Or is the blame society's at large,
Should you give them some free assistance,
Or have police put them on a charge?

Unlike the good samaritan,
You choose to walk on the other side,
Quite happy to debate lofty moral issues,
Until you meet reality, stumble and collide.

Cardboard City's inhabitants,
Are surely past redemption,
Would you really make that statement,
If in there lived *your* son?

Shouldn't they help themselves more?
Perhaps they've already been trying,
All I know is they are fellow human beings,
And in the winter ... they are dying.

ENTRANCED

Oh Golden globe;
Far out to sea,
You seem to beckon;
Call out to me,
You light a path
For me to follow,
Your voice is warm,
Not cold or hollow,
Though sorely tempted,
I must decline,
But wait once more
For you to shine.

The clouds moved by,
The wave crests danced,
But I couldn't leave;
For I was entranced ...

FALL LIKE A FEATHER

You must fall like a feather
And bounce like a ball,
If people cut you short
You must stand really tall.

If kicked while you're down
Make sure that you get up,
Show you're a dog with teeth
If they whip you like a pup.

If they dampen your spirit
Show your hope is still dry,
If clouds cover your parade
Make your *fly-pass* extra high.

If hit hard below the belt
Smile and shake their hand,
If your life goes off course
Just imagine it was planned.

Flex and bend like a willow
But retain a heart of oak,
If someone upsets you
Try and treat it as a joke.

You must fall like a feather
And bounce like a ball,
And - always come out fighting
When your back's against the wall.

I ONCE HAD A RELATION-SHIP

I once had a relation-ship,
But she sailed far away,
Up anchored and set course to find
Another sheltered bay.

Our stormy and tempestuous affair
Had ended, sunk at last,
The current which pulled us apart,
Had run so strong and fast.

She didn't even wave, but left me
At low ebb, high tide,
Her face was stern, my head was bowed,
My salty tears to hide.

My flag alas, she flies no longer
From her stately mast,
Our swell affair was present tense,
But sadly now 'tis past.

She left full speed ahead, her sails
A'billowing like a cloud,
If happiness equals silence,
My heartbreak's cannons loud!

I stare from port, my eye on a star,
Bored, like a boat without rudder,
My emotions beached on a lonely shore,
Left to flounder and shudder.

A vessel like her will shore-ly land
Another love-struck fool,
I'm only one fish in a big big sea ...
And her heart is fathoms cool!

YE KNOW NOT WHEN

Tick-tock and then chime;
Our *life-clock* beats
Our precious time out,
As it slowly depletes.

No-one can know when
Their own *clock* will stop,
Will it end on a tick ...
Or will it end on a tock?

Each hour on the dot
Our clocks clearly chime,
To remind us all
Of our passing time.

Use your time wisely,
For *ye know not when,*
As engraved on the sun-dial;
On the church at St Wenn.

IN THE QUIET OF THE NIGHT

In the quiet of the night,
Where darkness steals the need for sight,
When most are asleep, I lie awake,
Waiting for the dawn to break,
Long past trying to count sheep,
My brain's shallow, but my thoughts are deep,
My mind's trying to put the world to rights,
But I think it might take ... several nights!

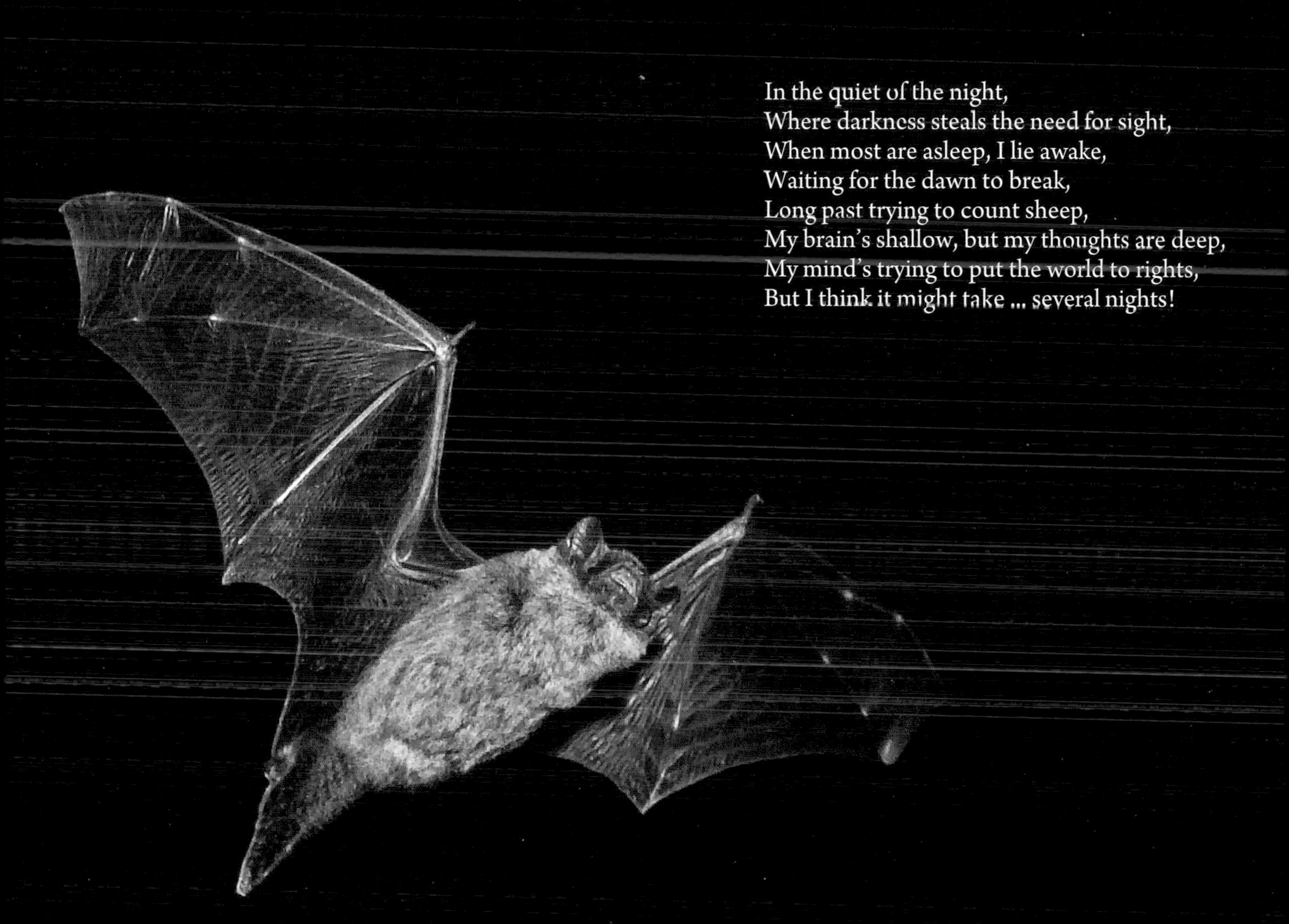

MY D FENCE

There's a fence all around me,
It keeps people away,
It gives me space of my own,
It keeps others at bay,
I constructed it myself,
It's the price I must pay.

It goes up for a mile,
While still touching the ground,
People have searched for a way in,
But one has never been found,
It's an impenetrable barrier,
That no sledge hammer can pound.

Does it make me feel claustrophobic,
Or does it make me feel secure,
Once I knew all the answers,
But now I'm not so sure,
Shall I make a hole in my fence,
Shall I fill it with a door?

Here I am stuck
In a defensive retreat,
I once so craved victories,
But I feared more a defeat,
Should I tunnel under my fence,
Should I dig really deep?

Should I stay here in my cocoon,
Or should I go out and explore,
Should I try again to embrace life,
Even though I failed once before,
Shall I cut a hole in my fence,
Need I bother fill it with a door?

My fence was to keep others out,
But it is both friend and foe,
For it also keeps me in,
When all I want is to go,
Shall I place explosives around it
And wait for it to blow?

All right you win, I'm coming out,
Waving a white flag up high,
I hope I fare better this time,
'Cos I'm reaching for the sky,
I'm taking off my lead boots,
This time ... please help me to fly!

CONFORM TO THE NORM

My Baby:
Don't be too quiet, yet don't be too shrill,
Don't be too restless, but neither too still,
Please grow up hardy, yet soft to the touch,
Not seeking too little, nor asking too much.

My Child:
Don't be precocious, yet don't be too shy,
The middle-sized apple of your father's eye,
Don't be too forthright, nor keep to yourself,
Don't be too daring, but care for your health.

My Son:
Don't aim too high, nor get stuck in a hole,
Nor hang back if offered an uninspired role,
Please don't take the high road or even the low,
The main road is best, not too fast or too slow.

My Epitaph:
Here lies a man, who knew how to conform,
Who never left harbour, for fear of a storm,
Avoiding the hot and the cold for luke-warm,
In loving (but not too loving) memory,
Of your only son ... Norm.

OSTRI-SIZED

People call me ugly,
And other hurtful names,
I'm often ostri-sized,
My feathers used for games.

They say the *Ugly-Duckling*
Grew up to be a swan,
And tho' I'm still but very young,
They ask me *What went wrong?*
I'm left here on my own-some,
And feel so sad and blue,
Well you would feel the same
If you were an ... *emu*.

ONE DAY I DREAMED

One day I dreamed ...

There was no longer any *Third World,*
Just a united *First,*
Famine clearly vanquished forever,
And no-one died of thirst.

Power was never used to enslave,
And wars were fought no more,
Man's resources were pooled together,
To help aid all the poor.

Man respected his fellow creatures,
Living in harmony,
The oceans free from all pollution;
Helped by *green* energy.

People didn't need to live in fear;
Crime a thing of the past,
A planet no longer fragmented;
A one-peace world at last.

I awoke in time to catch the news;
News of crime, famine, war,
Moist-eyed I headed back to my bed,
To try and dream ... some more!

LET ME SAIL AWAY FOREVER

Let me sail away forever,
Let me cast off from the shore,
Let the swirling mists engulf me,
Till reality rules no more,
Let me sail the mighty oceans,
Let me pass by cliffs anew,
Let me navigate a passage,
Through the rolling veil of blue,
Let my anchor never hold me,
Let my sails always billow out,
Let me sail away forever, and
May I never turn about.

MOSS-HOLE BOUND

I heard a noise ...
Could that be food?
I peer outside;
I'm really shrew-d,
My sight is dim,
But I am not,
Though small, I'm fierce,
And hunt a lot,
So stand aside,
I'm coming out,
Don't bar my way ...
Or I'll sort you out!

POWER TO THE PEOPLE

Monolithic steely strides;
Cable strains while nature hides,
Arms outstretched from metal sides,
A buzzard glares as by he glides.

A pylon dwarfs a nearby tree,
But makes no home for bird nor bee,
Landscape ruined, just so that we
In idle warmth ... can watch TV!

THE LIGHT

A Light so brilliant;
It can break the blackest dark asunder,
A Light so powerful;
It can out-strike lightning in full thunder,
A Light so glorious;
It can fill all who see it with wonder.

And ...

Although so very bright;
Its rays will never blind,
Although always present;
It is not easy to find,
Although it is so mighty;
It is gentle as can be,

And if anyone were to follow it,
It would show them ... Eternity.

THAT LIFE WAS MINE

That life was born in Africa,
In a poor, dusty, rural part,
His parents had few possessions,
He only desired their heart.

That life fought hard against disease,
Which time after time, nearly won;
His parents' love saved him, urged him to fight,
Just as they had done.

That life suffered terrible hunger and thirst,
As famine and drought were neighbours;
He worked with his parents whilst very young,
Undaunted by childhood labours.

That life lived through civil wars; he lost
Two cousins and one best friend;
The hatred he could not understand,
He prayed for the fighting to end.

That life gained an education, determined
To try to break the mould;
The treasure he knew could be found within,
Not panned for, like fool's gold.

That life then studied medicine,
A doctor's arduous training,
Wanting to bring relief and care
To all the poor there, still remaining.

That life stepped onto a land-mine . . .

COLOUR FADING NEVER

Picked from the garden of life,
As unique as any flower,
As beautiful as a rainbow,
Trapped in an April shower.

Like a blossom pressed and dried,
Its colour fading never,
I have pressed you
Between the pages of my life,
Where I hope you will stay forever.

SASQUATCH

The Abominable Snowman
May try to melt into obscurity,
Yeti remains a glittering star
On the ecological ladder,
After a very, very long climb.

Yes indeed:
Bigfoot is a leg end
In its own time!

YIG AND YOG

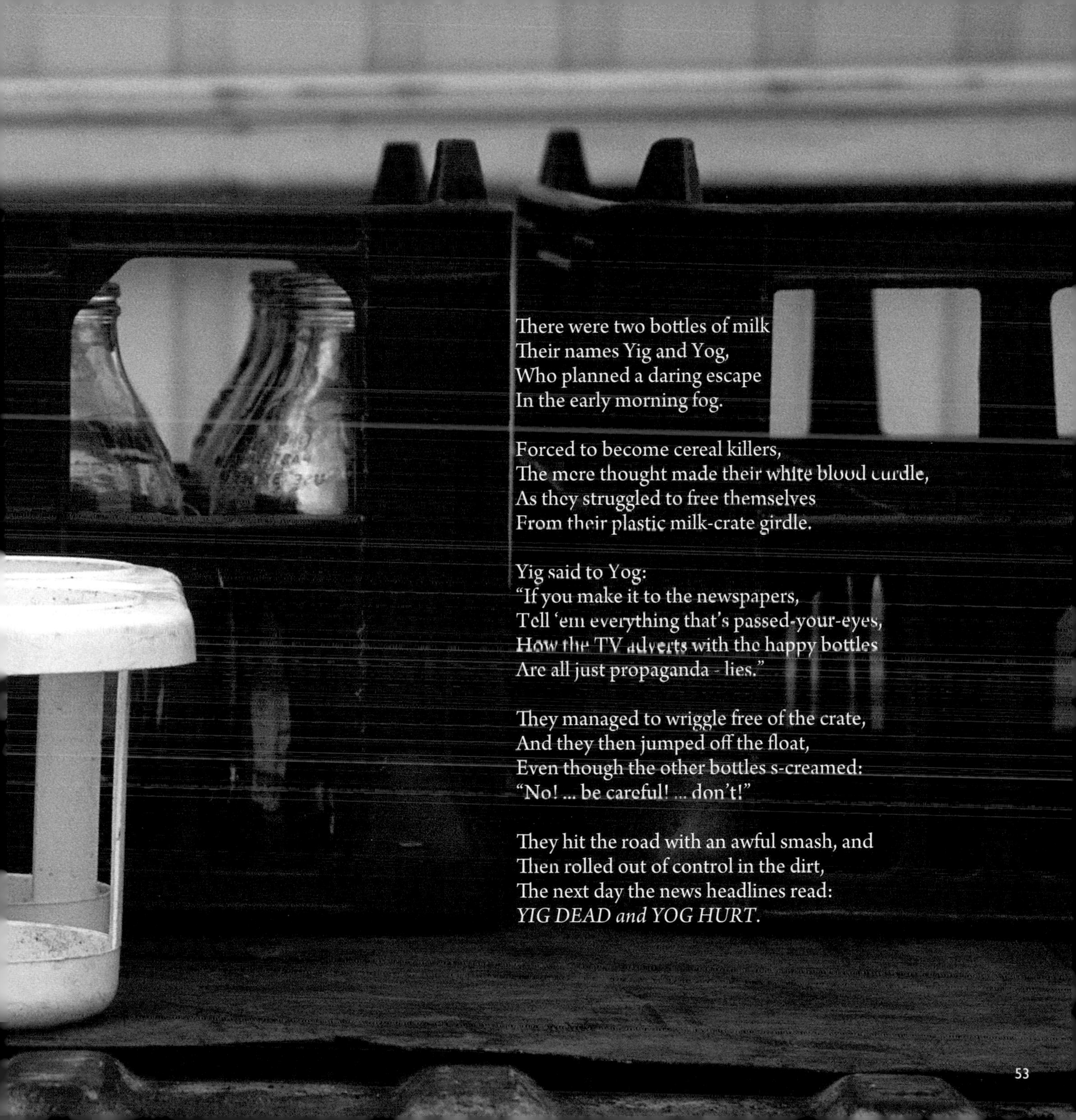

There were two bottles of milk
Their names Yig and Yog,
Who planned a daring escape
In the early morning fog.

Forced to become cereal killers,
The mere thought made their white blood curdle,
As they struggled to free themselves
From their plastic milk-crate girdle.

Yig said to Yog:
"If you make it to the newspapers,
Tell 'em everything that's passed-your-eyes,
How the TV adverts with the happy bottles
Are all just propaganda - lies."

They managed to wriggle free of the crate,
And they then jumped off the float,
Even though the other bottles s-creamed:
"No! ... be careful! ... don't!"

They hit the road with an awful smash, and
Then rolled out of control in the dirt,
The next day the news headlines read:
YIG DEAD and YOG HURT.

IT CERTAINLY WOULD

When the wisest man in the world said
"It would be a tragic shame if ever
The Great Forest were to be reduced
To a small clump of trees."
Everyone, without exception, answered
"It certainly would."

So when *The Great Forest*
Was eventually reduced
To a small clump of trees,
That is what they decided to call it ...
It Certainly Wood.

CORNWALL EXPLORED

Coastline, rocky, rugged, proud,
Crumbling cliffs in ozone shroud,
Sun-kissed drifts of desert sand,
Golden frame of a sea cradled land.

Fishing village, atmospheric hub,
Brass band playing, outside quaint old pub,
Boats, all sizes, rest near harbour wall,
Wading birds sift through tide-filled pool.

Foliage explosion of a Cornish hedge,
Country lanes snake, and young birds fledge,
Ruminants, punctuating, quilted hill,
Buzzards soar and wise hares are still.

Tin mine engine house, towering stack,
Roof caved in, gorse and bracken's back,
White clay peak, geometrical and sleek,
Earth's riches gouged, canyon deep.

Moorland, open, untamed, granite strewn,
Wild ponies dance to a skylark's tune,
Tor and beacon, barrow and mound,
You're in God's own country,
When you walk this ground.

CHRIS AND ALICE

My name is Chris,
Her name is Alice,
We're cocooned in
A plantastic palace,
While balanced on
The woodlands eaves,
We banquet on
What others leaves.

We're pillers of
Socie-eat-he,
We pay our debts
And dine for free,
But our sights are set
Up in the sky,
For we've been promised
One day we'll fly!

Smile
Denial

REQUIRED
NO MORE

Do you know what it's like
To be required no more,
To be put out to grass,
To be kicked out the door,
To know your work's ended,
No more will be done,
To be slung on the tip,
Pushed aside by the young,
To be pensioned off
In an unceremonious way,
To know you've had your's -
Every dog has its day,
To have an appetite for work,
But be left to hunger,
To be replaced by someone
More able and younger,
To be told you're too old,
When you feel in your prime,
To be sent on your bike,
Before it's your time,
To be all washed up
And flushed down the drain,
To have no physical wounds,
But still be in pain,
To feel your age,
Find you're no Peter Pan,
To see your life going
No longer to plan,
To recall when you felt rich,
But now you feel poor,
To hear your heart slowly pumping,
Alas it races no more,
To experience an emptiness
That nothing will fill,
To have no medical symptoms,
But still feel ill,
To be out of control
Of your own destiny,
To be constantly asking
Why me ... why me?

Do you know what it's like
To have your freedom back at last,
To be able to choose new colours
Once pinned out of reach to the mast,
To find tho' you've lost your employment,
You can still keep hold of your pride,
To discover the grass *is* greener
On the unexplored other-side,
To patch up your battered ego,
Once thought irretrievably torn,
To feel a strong urge to celebrate,
When others expect you to mourn,
To take a fresh look at careers,
When you thought it was all in the past,
To discover your destiny's liquid,
And never in concrete cast,
To realise your aspirations,
Which no more are held on ice,
To alter your life's ingredients,
And add a small pinch of spice,
To discover you're no longer frightened
By things that are different or new,
To embrace all those sensible changes,
And take a much loftier view,
To keep everything in context,
And never let monsters appear,
To look to your dreams and take aim,
Keeping your sights crystal clear,
To be intimidated no longer
By applicants younger than you,
To know a wise captain will always
Choose an experienced crew,
To retain your sense of adventure,
Your instinctive love of fun,
To put down the now closed chapter,
And enjoy the one just begun,
To be welcomed back to life's table,
And invited to sit down and dine,
To feast till you're utterly bloated,
And swill it all down with sweet wine.

THE INVINCIBLE BIRTHDAY CANDLE

'The Greatest ... the Most Superb ...
The Invincible Birthday Candle ..!'
It was at the peak of its career,
It was much too hot to handle.

Its boasts always waxed, never waned,
It made the other candles sick,
Its bragging claims enough to get on
A more modest candle's wick.

No challenger came forward ...
Though not through lack of spine,
They just watched and waited,
Preferring to bide their time ...

Night after night, it would bluster away:
"On me, no other candle is a patch,"
Then one day it was stuck into a cake,
And it finally met its match.

RAINDROPS DESCEND

Raindrops descend, puddles form,
A stream engulfed, a river is born,
A course is set, the sea to reach,
Meandering ponderously to a far off beach.

The sea reclaims its myriad young,
Kidnapped by clouds, thunder-slung;
The storm is long past with calm all around;
Albatross glide, with a whisper of sound.

Seagulls circle, dogfish sleep,
Gannets dive and dolphins leap,
But black clouds return and lightning flashes
Over storm-tossed seas, as thunder crashes.

Once more a stealthy cloud abducts infant water,
The sea's own offspring: a son ... a daughter;
The thief sets off at a wind blown pace,
The anguished mother unable to chase.

The criminal finds refuge in a partisan crowd,
A formless body in a vaporous shroud;
The cloud has no guilt, shows no remorse,
But heads inland on a predestined course.

A hill stands guard, like a customs post;
It stabs the guilty, but allows past the host;
The rogue cloud is ruptured, severed seam and pleat,
Releasing its captives and accepting defeat.

Raindrops descend, puddles form,
A stream engulfed, a river is born,
A course is set, the sea to reach,
Meandering ponderously to a far off beach ...

DARKENED ROOM

Have you ever sat and pondered
In a darkened room;
Reality melting away
In the murky gloom,
Ignoring gravity's attempts
To try and hold you tight,
Heading off into space on a
Magic-carpet flight?

Did you explore the Universe,
Travel through all time,
Contemplate your own existence;
Even think of mine?

Did you ever find the answer,
To the question *Why?*
Did you really want to return from
Flying through the sky?

Did you come back with a jolt when
Someone came in the room,
Did the bright light startle you;
Did reality resume?

PL ... EASE

Don't see only our disabilit ... ease,
Don't deny us basic facilit ... ease,
Don't ignore our many abilit ... ease,
Don't compound our varied difficult ... ease,
Deal head-on with the harsh realit ... ease.

You never know what life has in store,
You may fall one day and rise no more,
You may join our ranks, afraid, unsure,
You may write words to plead; implore.

We are not an alien race,
We have a voice, we have a face,
We have our part to play; a place.

Let us join life's lively dance,
Let us have an equal chance.

Pl ... ease.

THE AGE OF INNOCENCE

The age of innocence,
A daughter we adore,
Long hot summer days,
A toddler only four.

Tadpoles in a jam-jar,
Watching as they wriggle,
Nature being studied,
Inviting her to giggle.

Eyes filled with laughter,
No clouds hide the sun,
Happiness a toddler's gift,
Enjoyed by everyone.

Wide-eyed and innocent,
To her, life's one big game,
If only we could join her ...
Be innocent once again.

WEDDING VOWS

May we forever be lovers,
May we forever be friends,
And should we hurt each other,
May we quickly make amends.

May we enjoy our passion,
But never let compassion die,
Thinking in selfless terms as *we*,
Never emphasising *I*.

May we forever be soul-mates,
May our love eternally last,
May the food of love sustain us,
May we never have to fast.

May we use each other's strengths,
When we are feeling weak,
May we both learn to compromise,
And always as one voice speak.

May we never keep dark secrets,
May we never tell each other lies,
May we both work unceasingly,
To ensure our love never dies.

MEMORY OF
CATHERINE
Wife of
WILLIAM KERSLAKE
of Race-hill Launceston,
Who died Feb 20 1863
AGED 36 YEARS.
The Lord gave, and the Lord hath taken

RESTING IN PEACE

Life's hustle and bustle has ended,
Now I've passed away, deceased,
My new terra firma home,
A guarantee of eternal peace;
Never disturbed by clamour or noise,
I don't even hear a sound,
In this world unknown to the living,
Within the ravenous ground,
No one here is the least impressed
By status, rank or class,
Deep below the skylit realms
Of fresh-green, new-mown grass.
The worms treat everyone the same,
Whether noble born or serf,

As I idle away my leisure hours,
Under neatly replaced turf,
No need ever to work again,
I've had my share of toil,
As my weary bones I rest forever,
Amidst the once feared soil,
I reflect on life's rich journey,
A long winding path, well-trod,
Time for contemplation assured,
Beneath the mounded sod,
This place is now home to me,
I don't think of it as a tomb,
Birth and death entwined as one,
In Mother Nature's womb.

THE BIRDS

The dawn broke;
Shattered beyond repair,
The birds spoke;
Chirps of joy, cheeps of despair,
The fog rolled;
But there was no dice in sight,
The birds strolled;
They were in no mood for flight,
The fog sank;
Once gone, would it be mist?
The birds preened;
Making their sleek bodies list,
The wind blue;
Colour blind though it was,
The birds flew;
Who knows why?
Just ... because.

DYMOND -
A GIRL'S WORST END

In early eighteen-forty-four,
In Cornwall's heart; on Bodmin Moor,
Charlotte Dymond, a young farm maid,
Had her throat slit with a steel blade,
She crossed fast streams and deadly bogs,
Found her way through mists and fogs,
But couldn't stop that fatal blow,
That stole her life and laid her low,
She walked to meet someone that day,
Just who that was ... no one would say,
Found days later beside a track,
Laid on a cart; her shroud a sack,
The surgeon, Thomas Good, was fetched,
Had in his mind, her white face etched,
Charlotte untouched by fox or crow,
Had she been moved ... he did not know,
No evidence was ever found,
But her young boyfriend had gone to ground,
Fingers so quick to point his way,
Matthew Weeks panicked; ran away,
The hapless cripple, was soon caught,
No other culprit was ever sought,
The judge was just a *rubber-stamp,*
Bodmin Gaol was dark and damp,
The scaffold built, the crowds arrived,
Matthew swore he had not lied,
The floor gave way, the rope drew tight,
Was justice done ... the verdict right?

GREEN CAR

A rover you were, all your working life,
But your conscience caught up with you,
You chose honourable re-tyre-ment and
You're now *green* through and through.

Once you greedily thirsted for petrol,
But finally kicked the habit,
And you now partake of fresh country air,
Just as rural as any wild rabbit.

In the past your throaty engine's roar
Out-decibeled the traffic's bustle,
But you now much prefer to listen to
The dry, restless leaves which rustle.

Alas your coachwork no longer gleams,
But you still retain all of your pride,
It's just your wish to be *at one* with nature,
As everything else you've tried.

A frosty morning is no deterrent,
To a well-seasoned convert like you,
It's just an unavoidable prelude,
To the sparkling spring-time dew.

Your days of *road rage* long since gone,
When you used to speed and scramble,
You're now content to pull to one side,
And be overtaken ... by a bramble.

LIFE'S GREAT POND

Even

the smallest

creature

makes ripples,

When it enters

Life's Great Pond.

And those ripples just

keep

on expanding -

Far, far, far beyond.

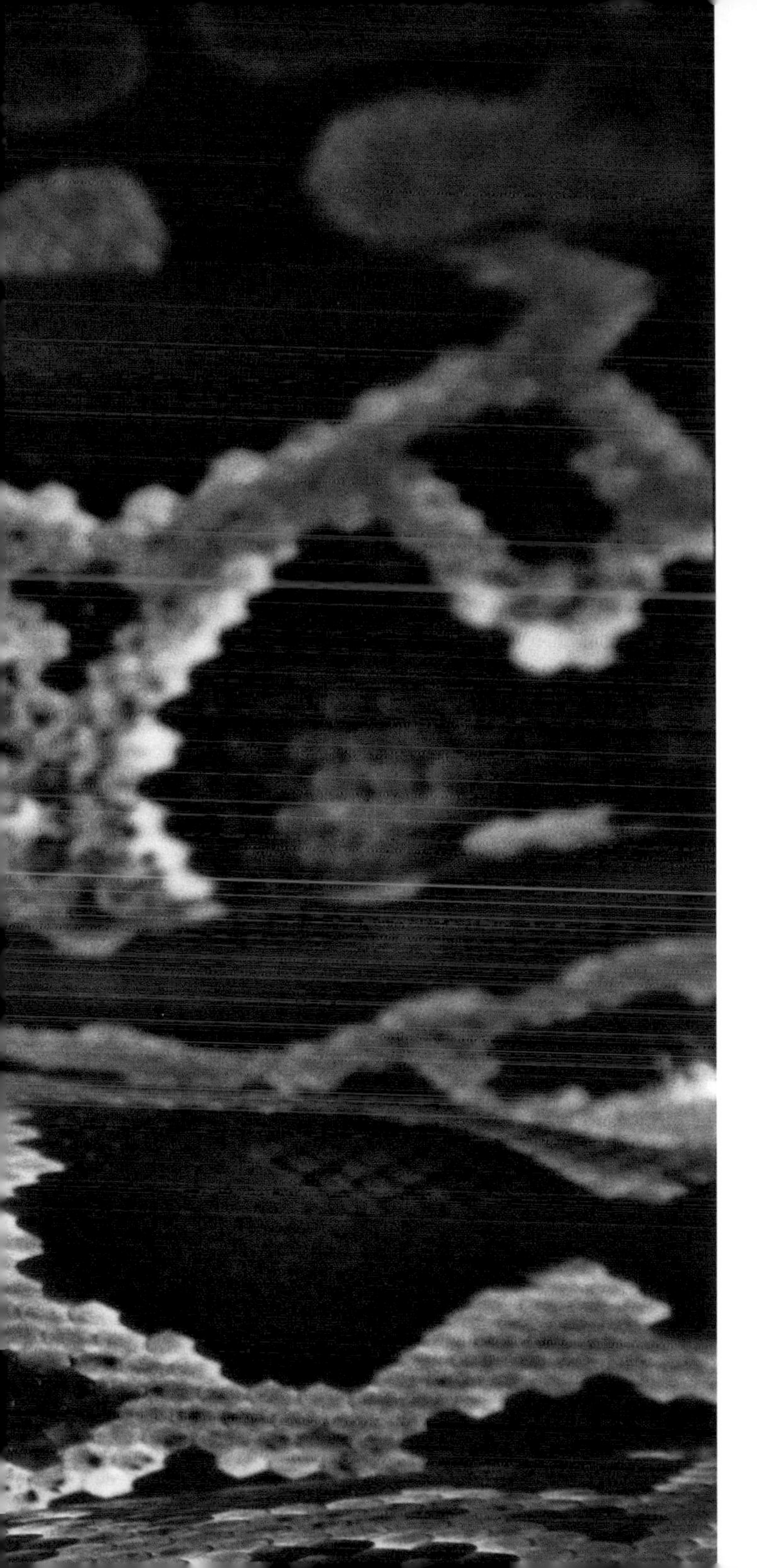

RE: COILS

What a great reptile,
A *Royal Python* - no less,
A serpent so dapper;
Never seen in a mess,
Non-poisonous, deaf, mute;
Except for its hiss,
It likes nothing more
Than to hug and to kiss!

Though it has no arms,
Harmless it is not,
Make no mis-snake a
Mean streak it has got,
Outside of its coils
The view is just fine,
But if invited inside
You'd be wise to decline!

Don't be enticed in
By its hypnotic stare,
For when those coils tense,
They act like a snare,
For those patterned coils;
Look brill' from without,
But lose their appeal
When wrapped
Around your snout!

MY MEADOW

Meadow quiet,
Meadow sweet,
Meadow flowers
At my feet.

Let me play,
Let me explore,
Let me stay
Forevermore.

LOVE AND FRIENDSHIP

Love and friendship makes
The world go 'round,
While hatred
Applies the brake.

Let's pray that love
Will long prevail,
If only for ...
God's sake.

TO HAVE AND TO HOLD

Confused by DVD interactivity,
Lost in soulless internet chatrooms,
Spied on by precision satellites,
Tracked down by mobile phone texters,
Hit by multi-media bombardment,
Tied up with twisted video tape,
Engulfed by ephemeral nothingness,
Brain awash with binary,
Consumed by CD ROM gigabytes.

Call me stuck in the past,
Say I'm not *cool*, but cold,
Because my ideal is a good book ...
To have and to hold.

ஹென்றி போர்டு மருத்துவமனை
HENRY FORD HOSPITAL
டாக்டர். D. சுரேஷ்வரிக்குமார். வியாழக்கிழமை உடம்பில் உள்ள மருவு அகற்றப்படும். Dr. D. SURESHWARI KUMAR.

BUT THIS IS AN EMERGENCY

Tell Dr Blood it's Mrs Bloomsberry;
He always sees me right away;
He's such a wonderful doctor - so much
Better than that Doctor Day.

What the devil are you incinerating,
I consider your tone a right cheek,
I've not bothered you for ages; I've
Not phoned for at least ... a week.

But this is an emergency;
Yes of course it's serious,
I'm sweating, shivering, sneezing
And feel quite delirious.

I'm running a terrible temperature,
I'm covered all over in spots,
My body aches from head to toe,
My muscles all tied up in knots,
My heart's got the palpitations,
Though I've got a pulse - it's quite weak;
My poor throat's ever so red and sore,
It's increasingly hard ... to ... speak,
My eyes are all glazed and weepy,
My ears are infected and blocked,
I think there's a chill in my kidneys
And my joints have all stiffened and locked.

My stools are alarmingly liquid,
My water's grey, misty and strong,
I'm suffering pins and needles, in fact ...
I don't think I've got very long.

He can see me on Thursday morning,
An appointment for half-past ten,
But that's no good at all to me ...
I'll be better again by then!

CHOSEN CHILD

Chosen Child, crowned this night,
Whilst fire-works light the sky;
Take over please as ruler now
Before we elders die.

We leave you all this Planet and
Dark Universe beyond;
Your word will travel far and wide,
Like ripples on a pond.

Our generation tires now,
The baton we pass on;
Please take it and run swiftly, for
The human-race goes on.

IT’S A STRESSFULL WORLD
WE LIVE IN

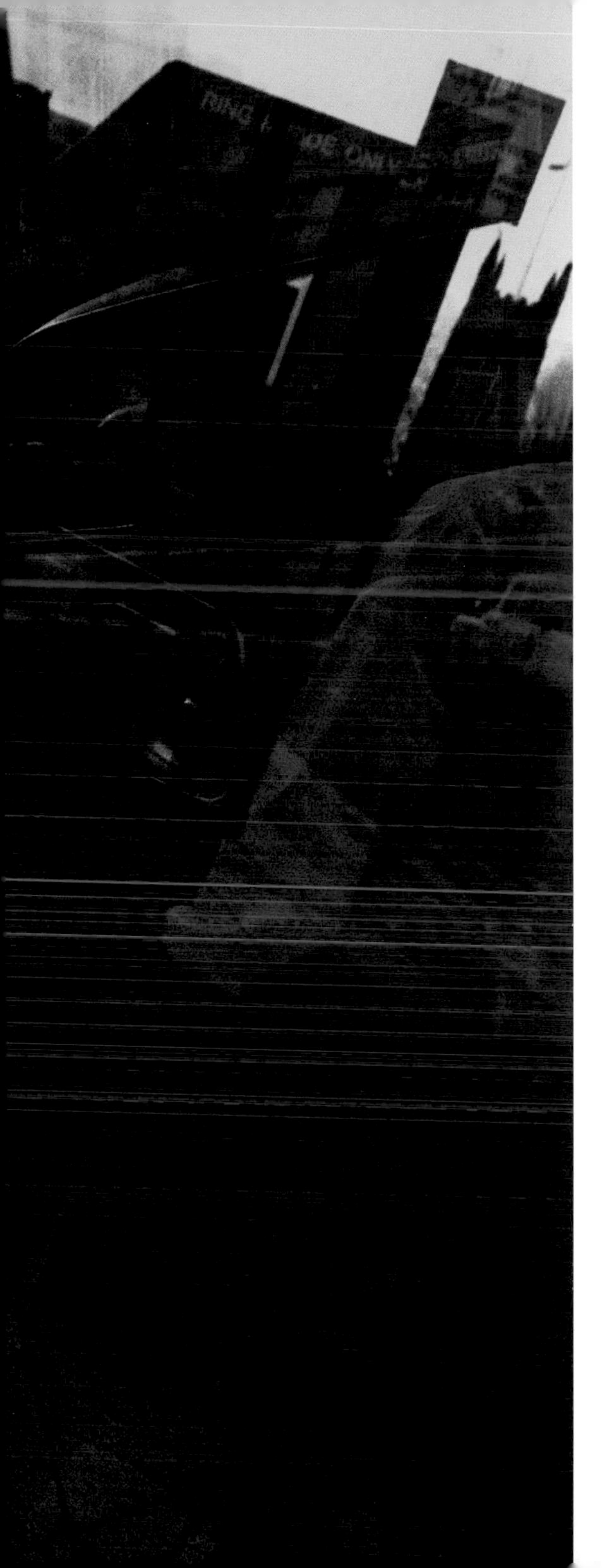

STRAIN is pressure on the muscle,
Stress is pressure on the brain,
A culmination of anxieties,
Hard to bear, hard to explain,
It's a stressful world we live in ...

PRESSURE on the muscle, is called strain,
Pressure on the brain, is called stress,
Over exertion of the grey matter,
Cerebral tiredness, mental duress,
It's a stressful world we live in ...

STRESS is pressure on the brain,
Strain is pressure on the muscle,
Symptoms of life's hectic pace,
Attempts to cope, with life's hustle and bustle,
It's a stressful world we live in ...

PRESSURE on the brain, is called stress,
Pressure on the muscle, is called strain,
Perhaps trying too hard to compete,
A desire too strong to attain,
It's a stressful world we live in ...

Don't expect too much from life,
While still always trying your best,
Put your shoulder against the wheel,
The strain in your muscle is real,
But leave all the stress for the rest!

IS THERE ANYONE FOR STUFFING?

"Is there anyone for stuffing?
Well done George, send us down your plate,
Auntie, if you've finished with the cranberry sauce
Could you please pass it across to Kate."

"Brian can I interest you in my brussels?
There's nothing quite like a good sprout,
If anyone wants anything passed,
Don't wait to be asked, just shout."

"Richard, will you please sit and eat,
And just stop irritating Claire,
No, you better wash your hands first,
You're getting gravy in her hair."

"Ted, you wanted more potatoes,
What, you only want one or two?
But the ones left really aren't that big,
I'd better pile on a few."

"Sarah, you're not looking after your young man,
The poor boy's been left to starve,
Go and get him some more turkey dear,
Your Father will help you to carve."

"Malcolm, not too much in Grandma's glass,
You know what she gets like,
Open another red for Father,
I'll stick to the bubbly-white."

"Well if everybody's had enough,
I think I'd better finish the peas,
Richard, don't cough over the table,
Remember your manners, please."

"Make way for Father and the Christmas pud,
I hope he hasn't overdone the brandy,
Saints preserve us ... Father's on fire!
Oh, well smothered dear, three cheers for Mandy,
Hip hip hooray,
Hip hip hooray,
Hip hip hooray."

"No Louise, you can't pull the crackers yet,
We're saving those for tea,
Richard, take that stupid tinsel off your head
And put it back on the tree."

Starving Third-World children appeared,
As the TV remote was scrolled,
Scrabbling in the dirt for food,
As if a grain of rice was gold.

"It almost puts me off my food,
Thinking of the less fortunate than me ...
Well done lads, pitch in, finish the pud,
There's plenty more desserts for tea."

CHRISTMAS GREETING

Oh robin you so symbolize,
The spirit of Christmas cheer,
The chirpy way you bob about
At this festive time of year.

A *Merry Christmas* we exchange,
Our eyes through holly meeting,
Worth more to me than worldly-goods,
That warm unspoken greeting.

SADLY THEY WEREN'T THERE

The deaf man heard the church bells ring,

The blind man led him there,

The arm-less put their hands together,

The leg-less knelt in prayer,

The mute's song filled the church with such joy,

There was no room for despair

And as for those sat in the empty pews ...

Sadly, they weren't there,

The deaf man heard God's mighty word,

The blind man saw the light,

The leg-less marched along with pride,

The arm-less joined the fight,

The mute sang lustily, joyfully bringing

The words of the Bible alive,

But as for those sat in the empty pews ...

Sadly, they didn't arrive!

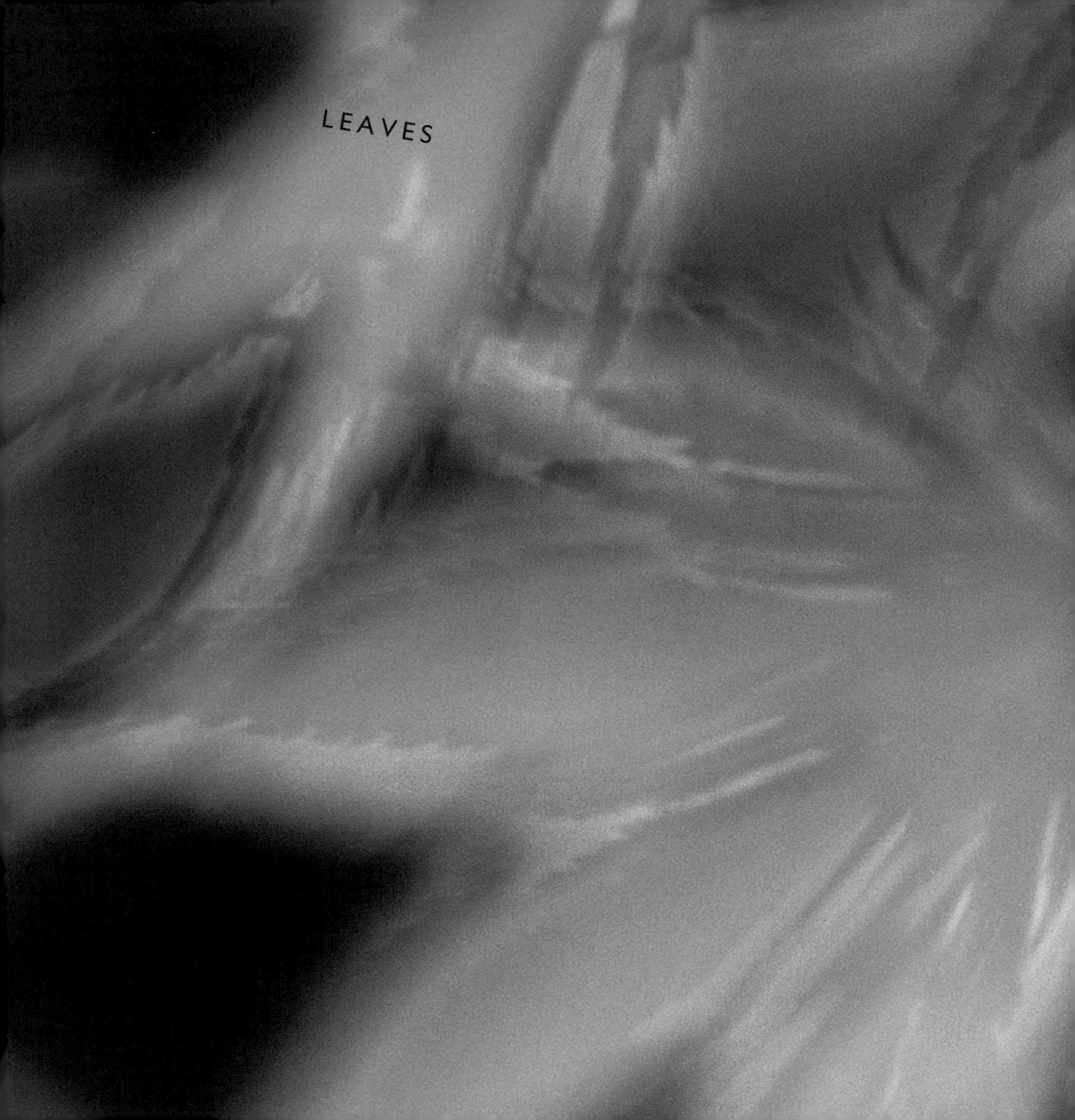
LEAVES

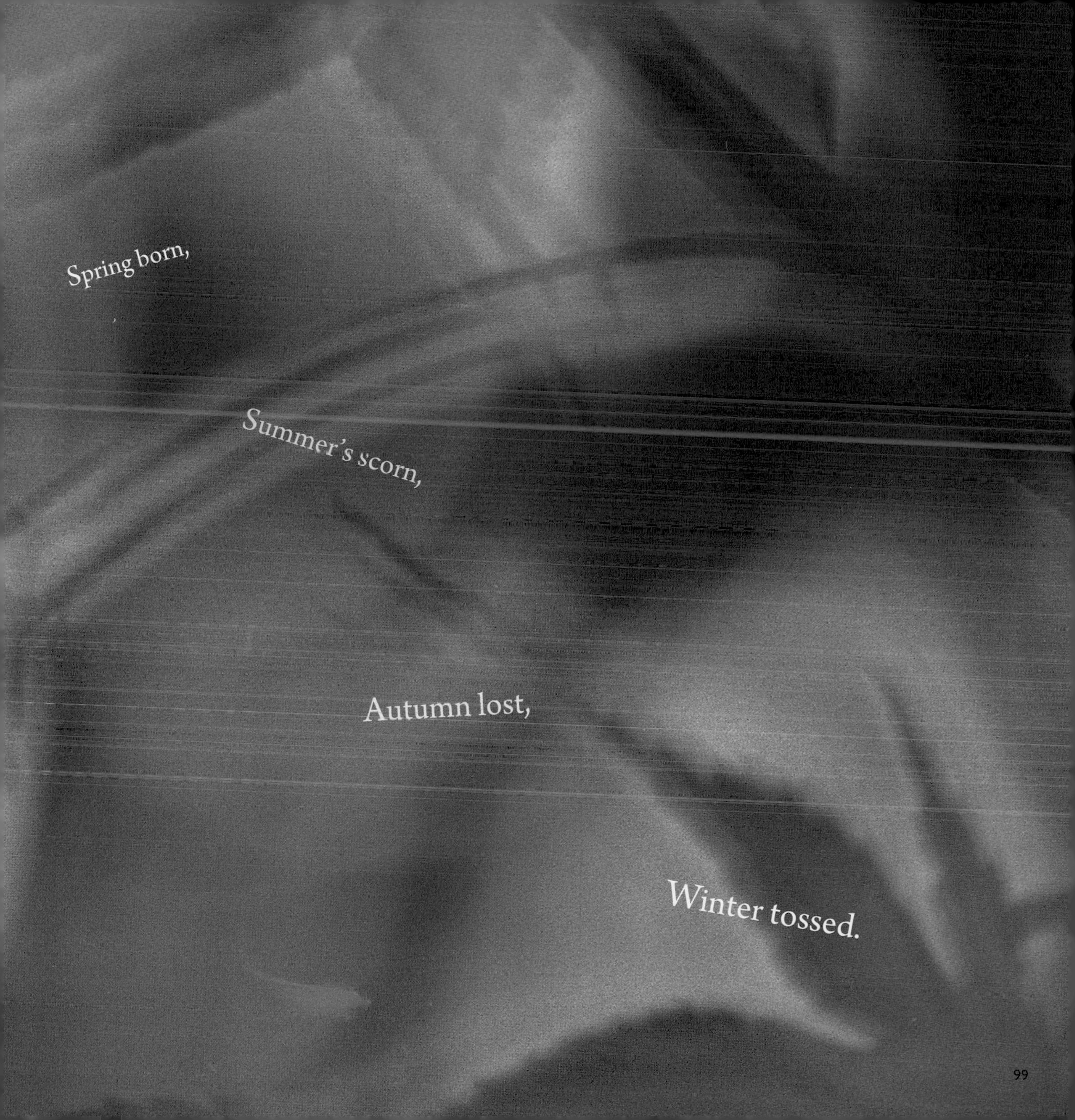

Spring born,

Summer's scorn,

Autumn lost,

Winter tossed.

UNCLE ALBERT

He was always known to everyone as *Uncle Albert,*
He used to sign all my birthday cards as *Uncle Albert,*
He used to turn around when I shouted *Uncle Albert,*
He was who we visited when we went to see *Uncle Albert.*

But I'm sorry to say, he's now belated,
Sadly passed away, dead and cremated.

And what I can't understand,
And what I am eager to learn,
Is why has everyone stopped calling him *Uncle Albert,*
And started calling him *Uncle Ern*?

THROUGH THE HOLE IN THE GLASS

Behind an old window,
A young girl often gazed,
Through a thin shattered pane,
Through a large hole unglazed.

Wistfully observing
The uncaring world pass,
Feeling invisible
To the more wealthy mass.

When life became too tough,
Her daydreams would unfold,
As protection against her
Brave hopes growing cold.

Where her mind could explore,
Expanding like light-gas,
And her thoughts could escape
Through the hole in the glass.

TOAD
IN
THE
HOLE

Though I'm ugly and I'm old
And I'm fat and I'm bald
And I'm grey and I'm cold;
I've still a story to be told ...

I've never been a handsome prince
As far as I can tell;
Unless I lost my memory
During a witch's evil spell!

I started my spawned life in a pond
In that valley, there beyond,
I haven't always been a *toad-in-the hole,*
I was once a cute tadpole.

I'm a source of fear for superstitious folk,
The hapless butt of many a joke,
I'm not endearing, or the least bit cute,
With all the charm of a hob-nail boot.

I'm not a worshipper of the sun,
My warty skin preferring it dank,
So I make my home in a shaded hole,
In a man-made stone hedge, or a bank.

You might think that I'm between a rock and a hard place,
That I've got my back to the wall,
But it's me that's never worked, paid tax or had a mortgage,
And never had to go to school!

THE BATTLE RAGED

The battle raged,
The arrows flew,
We were brave, but
We were few.

Out numbered,
Out fought,
Out flanked,
Out thought.

An arrow sought,
An arrow found,
I took the brunt,
I hit the ground.

In animate,
In pain,
In jured,
In vain.

Soldiers rarely say die,
Soldiers rarely grow old,
But my body grows weak,
But my body grows cold.

Ex pired,
Ex haled,
Ex tinct,
Ex ... *failed* ...

I'LL CARRI-ON REGARDLESS

Literary critics don't always like
The poetry what I do do,
They say it should all be recycled;
Flushed down the nearest loo ...
They say they cannot find a metre;
Although one works for the Water Board,
They dance all over my dignity;
My self-confidence they have floored,
They say me grammar is somewhat bad,
I think the word they used was *appalling*,
Their taloned claws grip sharpened knives,
They give me quite a mauling.

But kind, gentle reader (grovel),
I'm sure that at least you understand;
That my thoughts are erratic explosions
Not controlled, orderly or planned.

As long as my simple poems
Make you ponder, weep, or smile
I'll carri-on regardless,
For it would all have been worthwhile.

PS
My poetic aspiration
Is to become :
A Jack of all styles
And a master of pun.

HOLY
BIBLE

MY PRAYER

Dear Lord,

Don't let me ask only for myself,
For problems solved and better health,
Nor ask only for kin and friends,
With minor ills and moral trends,
But make me think in global terms,
Where drought kills and injustice burns,
Please tend to their greater needs first,
Help heal their wounds and quench their thirst,
My patient faith can wait till then,

My prayer sent -

Goodnight -

Amen.